American Community

Cow Towns

Raymond Bial

Children's Press®
A Division of Scholastic Inc.
New York   Toronto   London   Auckland   Sydney
Mexico City   New Delhi   Hong Kong
Danbury, Connecticut

Library of Congress Cataloging-in-Publication Data

Bial, Raymond.
 Cow towns / Raymond Bial.
   p. cm. — (American community)
 Includes bibliographical references and index.
   ISBN 0-516-23706-3 (lib. bdg.)   0-516-25075-2 (pbk.)
  1. Cattle drives—West (U.S.)—History—19th century—Juvenile
literature. 2. Cowboys—West (U.S.)—History—19th century—Juvenile
literature. 3. City and town life—West (U.S.)—History—19th century—
Juvenile literature. 4. Cities and towns—West (U.S.)—History—19th
century—Juvenile literature. 5. West (U.S.)—Social life and customs—
19th century—Juvenile literature. 6. West (U.S.)—History, Local—
Juvenile literature. I. Title.
 F596.B437 2004
 978'.02—dc22
                                                          2004005096

Cover design by Doug Andersen
Map by Robert Cronan
Photographs © 2004: Hulton|Archive/Getty Images: 29, 33; Kansas State Historical
Society, Topeka, Kansas: 16, 36, 37, 38, 39, 40, 42, 43 bottom, 43 top; Mary Evans
Picture Library: 8, 11, 35; National Geographic Image Collection/Bruce Dale: front
cover; Raymond Bial: back cover, 1, 4, 5, 6, 12, 13, 14, 15, 17, 18, 19, 20, 21, 22, 24,
26, 27, 31, 34; Wichita-Sedgwick County Historical Museum: 30.

Contents

Loading their belongings into Conestoga wagons, settlers moved westward to homestead farms, stake mining claims, or open stores in new towns.

Early Years

In the nineteenth century, hundreds of thousands of men, women, and children headed west in covered wagons or trains. On this long, dangerous journey, they crossed the Mississippi and Missouri rivers and then traveled over the vast stretches of the Great Plains. Longing for a better life, they **prospected** for gold in mountain streams, cut timber in sprawling forests, homesteaded on the prairie, or grazed herds of cattle on the open **range**.

Thousands of towns sprang up throughout the West—mining towns in the mountains, lumber camps in the deep forests, farming communities on the broad prairies, and cow towns on the rolling plains.

Townspeople provided goods and services for the miners, loggers, farmers, and cowboys. Merchants, hotel keepers, saloon keepers, bankers, shopkeepers, butchers, bakers, and schoolteachers—they all came and together transformed the West.

Here folks found high adventure. Some even struck it rich, then just as quickly lost a fortune—or their lives. But most simply wanted to make an honest living in a new place.

Cow towns sprang up throughout the West. They quickly drew many people who wished to start over by opening businesses on Main Street.

Cow towns became centers for trade and communications. Along with a stagecoach and a telegraph office, they had a depot where the railroad stopped.

Although these sturdy people came from many different places, they came to stay, and they became **boosters**, who promoted their town. As time went by, they united to deal with floods, droughts, tornadoes, and blizzards. Together they battled the epidemics and the fires that swept through their streets.

Among the most lively of these new communities were the cow towns, where cattlemen came to sell their herds. Texas longhorns were driven to these towns, loaded onto trains, and shipped to markets in the East. Most cow towns were in Kansas—Abilene, Caldwell, Dodge City, Ellsworth, Newton, and Wichita. However, early on, cattle were also driven up to Missouri—Kansas City, Sedalia, and Saint Louis. Cattle from the Dakota and Montana territories moved south along trails to Cheyenne, Wyoming, and Ogallala, Nebraska. There were railroad stations in many of these towns. Other towns, like Dallas and Fort Worth and Red River Station at the edge of Indian Territory, which is now Oklahoma, served as stopping points along the rugged trails.

In this engraving cowboys are driving a large herd of longhorn cattle north from Texas to the cow town of Abilene, Kansas.

Cattle Trails

Texas longhorns were descended from cattle brought over by the Spanish in the mid-1500s. Abandoned in the wilds of northern Mexico and Texas while ranchers went off to fight in the Civil War, the longhorns became a lean and hardy breed. With their long horns and sharp hooves, they could defend themselves against wild animals. And they were tough enough to withstand disease and drought. At the end of the Civil War, there were millions of these **ornery** critters. However there was little market for them in Texas, other than for **tallow** and hides.

During the Civil War, men had driven a few small herds of longhorns through Indian Territory to markets in Missouri and Illinois. After the war, if **cattle drivers** could move the cattle to Chicago, they could get as much as thirty-five to forty dollars a head—a large sum in those days. So in 1866 some ranchers set out on the first route, known as the Shawnee Trail and later as the Texas Trail or Texas Road. With the coming of the railroad, more trails were blazed into other states, especially Kansas.

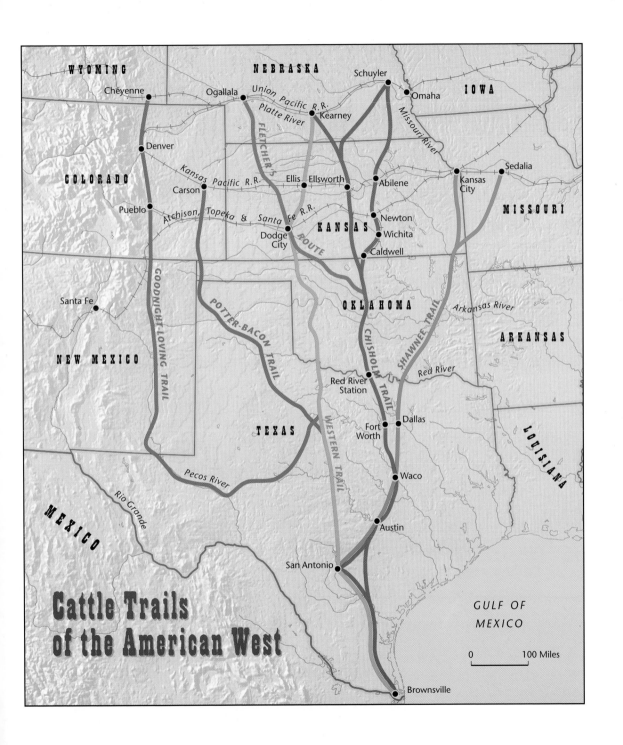

Cattle Trails of the American West

Git Along, Little Dogies

As I was a-walking one morning for pleasure,
I spied a young cowpuncher a-riding alone.
His hat was throwed back and his spurs was a-jingling,
As he approached me a-singing this song.

Whoopee ti yi yo, git along, little dogies,
It's your misfortune and none of my own,
Whoopee ti yi yo, git along, little dogies,
For you know Wyoming will be your new home.

Some fellows goes up the trail for pleasure,
But that's where they've got it most awfully wrong,
For you haven't an idea the trouble they give us,
As we go a-driving them dogies along.

Whoopee ti yi yo, git along, little dogies,
It's your misfortune and none of my own,
Whoopee ti yi yo, git along, little dogies,
For you know Wyoming will be your new home.

Running north from the grazing lands of Texas were the main trails for the long cattle drives: the Chisholm Trail, Fletcher's Route, the Goodnight-Loving Trail, the Shawnee Trail, and the Western Trail. Cowboys—who were also known as trail hands, drovers, and cowpokes—drove large herds through wide-open country. As one Texan said, "We went from the mouth of the Nueces River to Ellsworth, Kansas, without going through a gate." Of these routes, the Chisholm Trail became the most famous.

After the herd was settled for the night, cowboys unsaddled their horses, set up camp, and gathered around a fire as they ate their dinner.

Jesse Chisholm was born in 1805 of Cherokee and Scottish descent. In the 1820s Jesse came to Indian Territory, where he operated trading posts for forty years. As a freighter, he hauled goods along a route that became the Chisholm Trail. Known as a generous man, he died in 1868, and the inscription on his grave reads, "No one left his home cold or hungry."

As they tried to settle their jittery longhorns at night, the cowboys sang lullabies about this legendary route and their contrary cattle. "Git Along, Little Dogies" captures the spirit of the rugged cowboys who tended the herds as they made their way to the cow towns. (**Dogies** were not actually longhorn cattle but motherless calves.)

A Fresh Start

Starting a new town was not a simple task. An ambitious man known as a promoter hired surveyors to travel to a place on the plains where they laid out streets and lots for buildings and houses. The promoter then had to convince people to buy the lots, move to the middle of nowhere, and put up buildings in hopes that a town would prosper there.

The cow towns grew up along the railroads. When the transcontinental link was completed in 1869, thousands of miles of gleaming tracks stretched across North America. Between 1872 and 1890, Kansas spent over $18 million to support the construction of railroads in the state. Western migrants could settle just about anywhere, and many folks moved to one of the cow towns. As one Kansas land official said, it was a "day of great beginnings."

No one had ever seen anything like these towns. Under the bright sun of midday, dust blew around the sun-bleached wood-framed buildings, the creaky wooden sidewalks, the hitching posts, and the occasional water trough. At night the air rang with the laughter of rowdy cowboys and the mooing

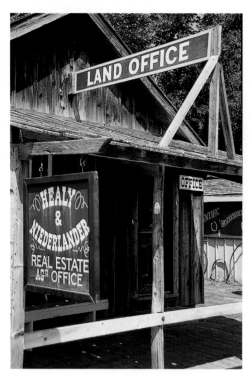

A group of surveyors laid out the communities and sold lots. Within a few years of the towns' birth, many—like Wichita and Abilene—flourished on the plains of Kansas.

For a while the buildings appeared freshly painted, new, and quiet—until rowdy cowboys drove herds of cattle down the dusty streets.

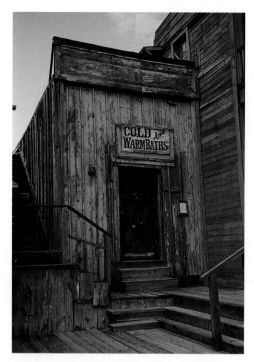

After weeks on the trail, the men who poured into the cow towns looked forward to baths and beds, although the rooms weren't always the best.

of cattle. Sometimes as many as 30,000 longhorns flooded a little town of 500 people.

To the ranch owner and beef buyer, the cow town was a place where they could make a twenty-thousand-dollar deal on a handshake. Railroad owners, whose freight trains were rolling west with full loads and often returning empty, could now haul cattle back to Chicago, which was the center of the meat packing industry. To the cowboy, who had been breathing trail dust and camping out in the wild, the cow town was a glorious place. He could get a shave, a haircut, and a bath. He could gamble a few nickels of his scant wages on a simple game of horseshoes or he could lose the whole wad in a single game of poker. And he could sidle into the saloon for a glass of cheap whiskey—even though the whiskey often tasted so bad that it came to be known as "Kansas sheep dip."

In 1867 Abilene was the first of the cow towns to enjoy the glory days of the big drives. That year Joseph G. McCoy established a **shipping yard** in the six-year-old town to pen three thousand cattle. He later wrote that Abilene was "a very small, dead place, consisting of about one dozen log huts—

low, small, rude affairs, four-fifths of which were covered with dirt for roofing; indeed, but one shingle roof could be seen in the whole city."

McCoy began putting up a three-story hotel, a bank, and a livery stable. While these buildings were still underway, he sent a man named W. W. Sugg south into Indian Territory, to let the cattlemen know about this wonderful new town. McCoy's shipping yard handled 35,000 cattle in its first year. Along with the longhorns came the cowboys, shooting and hollering with

In the early years of many cow towns, the houses and stores were log cabins, often with earthen roofs.

Pictured in this early photograph from 1858, Wild Bill Hickock was one of the most famous gunfighters in the West.

delight. They had wild times until Marshal Tom Smith tamed the town. With his bare fists, he punched out two rowdy cowboys by the name of Big Hank and Wyoming Frank and ordered them to leave town. Among the famous gunslingers who walked the streets of Abilene was the legendary Wild Bill Hickock. In 1871 Wild Bill succeeded Smith as Marshal.

Main Street

Most cow towns began as a collection of tents. Even though people had to sleep in the tents or covered wagons or out in the open, they were still full of energy and hope. A ramshackle collection of buildings soon sprang up. Builders used whatever materials were available—stone, logs, or slabs of **sod**. The log cabins and sod huts were replaced by frame buildings as soon as lumber, bricks, and window glass arrived by railroad from hundreds of miles away in the East. Seemingly overnight, buildings went up on the main street, which was usually broad, since teams of horses and wagons needed a lot of space to move up and down the street.

One of the first and most important businesses in town was the hotel. There, cowboys rented rooms and slept in soft beds after weeks of lying on the ground.

At first people didn't worry much about style. Most of the simple, rectangular buildings had wooden **false fronts** that that looked large and grand on the dusty street. The false fronts fooled no one, but they did provide space for signs on which businessmen could advertise their wares or services. Two-story buildings also had an outside staircase, which was simpler and cheaper to build than an inside one. It also saved room and provided a separate entrance to the second-floor quarters. The fronts of the buildings often had porches, which sheltered passersby from the rain and provided shade from the sun. Their pillars could be used for tying up horses, but there were also hitching posts and water troughs along the street. Raised wooden sidewalks often ran along the fronts of these buildings to keep people's feet above the dust or the knee-deep mud during rainstorms.

Among the very first buildings to go up was the hotel for the cowboys who drove the herds of longhorn cattle to town. So, the hotel keeper was among the first to arrive. People also established boardinghouses to provide rooms for the swarms of cowboys who rode into town from March to December.

Inside the dimly lit saloon, cowboys gambled away their wages in card games, roulette, and other games of chance.

The other most important businesses in town were the blacksmith shop and livery stable. Here a cowboy could have his horse fed, watered, sheltered, and re-shod. After taking care of his mount, he headed to the barber. A cowboy could get a bath here—his first in weeks.

Along with the hotels, boardinghouses, and livery stables, a town needed plenty of saloons to ease the parched throats of the cowboys—and various entertainments, such as dancing and gambling. Abilene, which had a year-round population of

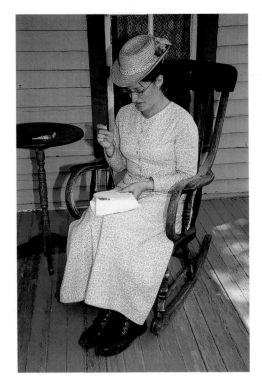

Women were needed in the cow towns, especially hard workers with independent spirits who were willing to manage their homes.

just eight hundred in 1871, had eleven saloons to serve the five thousand or more cowboys who brought the herds up from Texas each year. Gamblers and gunslingers also hung out in these places. Shooting was more likely to break out in the saloons than anywhere else in town.

The town also had a bank made of solid brick to assure depositors that their hard cash or gold dust was safe from robbers. There was a general store, or **mercantile**, an early version of a department store. Almost every cow town had a telegraph office and its own newspaper. As journalist Albert

Many people who moved to the cow towns raised families. Children went to one-room schools near their homes.

Cow towns also relied on businesses that looked after horses, such as harness and saddle shops, which specialized in leather goods.

Towns were fortunate if they had a good doctor to care for the ill and injured. Often doctors relied on drugstore medicines or home remedies.

Every town had to have a livery stable. There, horses were shod and boarded when people came to town for business or a little fun.

Richardson said, the newspaper was "mother's milk to an infant town." The newspaper not only allowed folks to keep up with the news, but also printed advertising posters for local businesses. Over time, townspeople built wood-framed houses on the side streets, along with schools and churches.

A growing community had a drugstore, barbershop, meat market, bakery, restaurant, and maybe even a photography studio. Towns had skilled craftsmen—tailors, shoemakers, hatters (makers of men's hats), milliners (makers of hats for women), and cabinetmakers. But there was often a shortage of good doctors. Many doctors who moved west did so because they did not have the skills to practice medicine back east. These doctors were not well qualified to treat the frequent injuries and illnesses of the townspeople. And there were many concerns about health.

Drinking water often came from polluted streams, and sewage was dumped right onto the street. The manure of horses, cattle, and chickens attracted swarms of flies. When the wind was right, a traveler could smell a town from a long way off. The *Wichita Eagle* newspaper reported on the odors of a particularly warm spring day, "A tall man who was sitting on the sidewalk said, as he got up and passed through noting with his nose, that there were two hundred and forty distinct and odd smells prevailing then and there." The newspaper then added more seriously, "All agree that some sanitary measures are needed, and heavy fines should be imposed on those who throw slops, old meats and decaying vegetable matter at their doors or on the street."

General Store

At the heart of Main Street was the general store. Here people looked over the shelves packed with goods and caught up on gossip by the potbellied stove and the cracker barrel. Sitting in chairs around the stove, where "every item of news" was shared, they idled away their time. Merchants usually welcomed these good friends and steady customers. But one complained in a local newspaper, "I am a storekeeper, and am excessively annoyed by a set of troublesome animals, called Loungers, who are in the habit of calling at my store and there sitting hour after hour, poking their noses into my business."

The general store did well as long as the cow town boomed. In 1864 William S. "Doc" Moon established his Frontier Store in a log cabin in Abilene. The town was just four years old, with 40 or so inhabitants and only 443 people in the whole county. Then the Kansas Pacific Railroad came to town, along with herds of longhorns and cowboys. Doc soon prospered, as did the many other stores that opened along Main Street.

The owner of the general store stood behind the counter and gladly accepted payment from his customers for groceries, hardware, and other goods.

Doc's store offered merchandise to satisfy just about every need of the cowboys, the townspeople, and the farmers who lived in the region: sugar and salt, molasses and meat, gunpowder and ammunition, coffee and cloth. On either side of the door, the windows were crammed with goods. Inside, the dim interior was filled with a blend of the pleasant odors of coffee, cheese, and tobacco, as well as the leather of new boots. One side was piled with dry goods, bolts of cloth, ready-made clothing, and hardware. On the other side the shelves were stacked with groceries. Hams, slabs of bacon, and pots and pans hung from the rafters. Barrels and kegs of pickles, vinegar, flour, sugar, and molasses stood on the floor. On the counters there were glass jars of striped candy canes and peppermint balls.

Fort Dodge was established in 1865 on the Arkansas River in southwest Kansas to guard the river crossing at the boundary of the Osage Indian reservation. In 1872—when the Atchison, Topeka and Santa Fe Railroad came through—several merchants, including Robert M. Wright, established Dodge City about five miles east of the fort. Within a month tents

The counters and shelves inside the general stores were jammed with a wide variety of goods—everything from food to clothing.

were replaced by frame houses and false-fronted stores along Front Street. "Business began, and such a business!" Wright later wrote in his memoirs. "Almost any time during the day, there were a hundred wagons on the streets. Dozens of cars a day were loaded with hides and meat, and dozens of carloads of grain, flour, and provisions arrived each day. . . . I never saw any town to equal Dodge." The hides and meat came from buffalo, and the first winter as many as 200,000 buffalo hides were shipped to tanneries in the East. However within a few seasons the buffalo were wiped out, and Dodge City became a cattle town. The first herds of cattle began arriving in 1876. And cowboys raised more hell in Dodge City than in any of the other cattle towns.

Dodge City was not only near the Chisholm Trail, it was farther west than any other Kansas town. Robert M. Wright took Henry M. Beverley, a good-natured Texan, as his business partner in his general store. Known as the Judge, Beverley had been a trail hand and was popular with the cowboys. "The Texas drovers seem to think a heap of the 'Old Jedge,'" wrote the *Dodge City Times*. Moreover every season

Wright, Beverley & Company sent agents deep into Texas to promote the advantages of Dodge City as a shipping point and entertainment center. The free-spending cowboys made Dodge City one of the wildest towns of the West. By 1882 cowboys drove 500,000 cattle to town. The cowboys quenched their thirst at one or more of fourteen saloons with names like Lone Star and Long Branch. And when the cowboys came to town, Wright's store prospered.

As shown in this picture of Texas longhorns being driven into Dodge City, towns really came alive when large numbers of cattle and cowboys arrived.

This early photograph shows the people and buildings on the main street of Wichita, Kansas, as they appeared in 1875.

Law and Order

Townspeople usually tried to "live and let live" when the trail hands arrived with the herds. When the railroad reached to Wichita in the early 1870s, it became the "Cowboy Capital." Its motto soon became "Everything Goes in Wichita!"

But folks still worried about dangers in their community. Between 1867 and 1871, more than a half-million cattle were shipped east from Abilene, and as many as five hundred cowboys were being paid off at a time. A law-abiding man in Newton, Kansas—about twenty-five miles north of Wichita—noted that saloons accounted for much of the town's size. Guns were constantly fired, reminding him of a Fourth of July celebration. "There was shooting when I got up and shooting when I went to bed."

Cow towns also attracted dangerous **outlaws**. Back east these violent men became the subject of widely read paperbacks known as **dime novels**, which glorified gunfighters and gamblers. Later, Westerns became popular as movies and television shows. These "shoot-'em-ups" portrayed a Wild

Cow towns also attracted plenty of dangerous outlaws. Wanted posters were often tacked on a wall of the sheriff's office.

West in which there was no law except that of the gun. Much of this was myth, but not all the stories were invented. Wanted posters were tacked onto buildings in town, and a number of gunslingers achieved fame, not for good deeds but for how many men they had killed, often in cold blood. Outlaws swaggered down the streets—Frank and Jesse James, the Younger brothers, and many others. Each was famous for his quick draw and his mean streak, and died young.

Law and order would come to the cow towns, but in the meantime guns blazed. Sometimes vigilantes hunted down horse thieves, cattle **rustlers**, and murderers, who were brought back to face a judge. Most often, however, these groups of self-appointed lawmen sought their own frontier justice and strung up the outlaw from the nearest tree in what was jokingly called a **"necktie social."** It required tough, brave men, such as U.S. marshals Wild Bill Hickock and Tom Smith—to bring justice to the towns and keep the peace.

So cow towns had a sheriff's office and jail, often with a nearby **gallows** casting a long shadow down the street. Though seldom a fancy building, the sheriff's office had a

Some of the most hated outlaws were cattle rustlers—like these masked gunmen on the plains of Nebraska—who stole cattle from ranchers.

central location on the main street. Inside was a sturdy jail where rowdy cowboys could sleep it off and outlaws could be held until they came before the judge (if they were lucky enough to have a trial). Frontier justice was swift and certain. Even when the outlaw was brought to trial, he was usually hanged from a rope noose conveniently located near the jail.

Many an unlucky cowboy was buried in the local cemetery, often called Boot Hill, where his grave was marked by a simple wooden cross.

Skilled carpenters earned a little extra money as coffin makers, hammering together rough wooden boxes.

Most every town had its Boot Hill, or graveyard, so named because men were often shot dead with their boots on. Each grave mound was marked with a wooden cross or rough board on which was scrawled the name of the deceased. Undertakers and grave diggers made a good living burying the dead.

Dodge City merchants certainly welcomed the cowboys' freely spending their money in the saloons and stores on Front Street, but not their reckless fighting. A visitor from Indiana later wrote in his hometown newspaper, "It is not true that the stranger in the place runs the risk of being shot down in cold blood for no offense whatever." But, Dodge City did, in fact, deserve its reputation for violence. Strangers were shot down for no reason often enough to keep law-abiding people off the street after dark.

Cowboys often got into fights in saloons. In these brawls they shot guns, threw punches, and smashed chairs over heads.

Along with Wyatt Earp and "Bat" Masterson, John Henry Holliday, better known as "Doc" Holliday, helped bring law and order to Dodge City.

By the early 1880s, a sign in Dodge announced that carrying firearms was forbidden, and lawmen required all visitors to surrender their "shooting irons" while in town. As one of the foremost leaders and merchants in town, Robert M. Wright agreed to hold these weapons, which were tagged and kept in his store. Wright commented on the large number of firearms: "At times they were piled up by the hundred."

Marshal Wyatt Earp certainly didn't hesitate to point the long barrel of his "Buntline Special" Colt revolver at the head of anyone who objected to the law. In Dodge City he made friends with Doc Holliday and Bat Masterson, who was later elected sheriff. In the Long Branch Saloon, Earp, backed by Bat Masterson, faced down Clay Allison, one of the most dangerous killers in the West. Earp exposed him as a coward and drove him out of town. Both Earp and Masterson soon moved on to other towns, and both outlived the Wild West—and the cow towns where they had once lived.

By late May 1885, the local newspaper in Dodge wrote, "The town is beginning to fill up with cowboys and stockmen. The saloons, gambling halls and dance halls are in full blast."

Many citizens were complaining to Governor John Martin about the cowboys' drinking, gambling, and shooting up the streets. The governor wrote to Robert M. Wright, who was then mayor, to express his concerns.

"You have been imposed upon by a lot of soreheads," Wright wrote back to the governor. "We have always been a frontier Town, where the wild and reckless sons of the Plains have congregated, their influences are still felt here, but we are rapidly overcoming them, let us alone and we will work out our own salvation in due season."

However the days of the cow towns—including Dodge City—were numbered.

The End of the Trail

As the herds of longhorns came into Kansas, farmers learned that the longhorns carried a tick that transmitted an infectious disease. Although sturdy Texas cattle were immune, the little bug caused a deadly "Texas fever" in Kansas cattle. Local farmers protested. They worried about the health of their

Seated on horseback, this cowboy watches over the herd in one of the last of the cattle drives, which would come to an end by 1885.

As more settlers in covered wagons poured into Kansas, they replaced the cowboys who had once come to town.

livestock. So, in 1869 the Kansas legislature established a **quarantine** line that confined the cattle drives to the largely unsettled western part of the state. They did not want their cattle to have any contact with Texas longhorns. Year after year, as more farmers settled in Kansas, the line was pushed westward. As were the railroads. The cattle herds and the cowboys followed them. One by one, the other cattle towns— first Abilene, which boomed for just four years, then Ellsworth, Wichita, and Ellis—were abandoned as shipping centers.

By 1880 the quarantine line would move far to the west. Farmers would run their fences across the Chisholm Trail, and the cattle drives would shift west to Dodge City. Located on the Santa Fe Railroad, Dodge City became the last and busiest of the cow towns. For ten years the town bustled: merchants filled their pockets with money, the Santa Fe Railroad loaded thousands of cattle onto its railroad cars, and folks laid to rest more than a few dead gunslingers in Boot Hill.

However more farmers were pouring into the region, and in 1885 the quarantine line ran along the western border of Kansas. To make matters worse, a great blizzard struck the plains in January 1886, killing cattle by the tens of thousands. The cattle industry in Kansas never recovered from this blow. The cattle drives to Dodge came to an end, and the town went into ten long years of poverty. During that time, many Front Street businesses failed. When the town again prospered it was because of sprawling farms of golden wheat and green alfalfa. Yet Robert M. Wright still boasted of his town, "Hurrah for little Dodge! She has a bigger heart, for her size, than any town in Kansas." But for the cow towns, it was the end of a fascinating time.

The settlers constructed sod houses for their growing families, dug through the tough prairie, and established prosperous farms.

The Old West Today

Farmers sold their crops and bought goods. Farming now kept the economies of the former cow towns alive.

The waves of western migration reached a peak in the late 1880s, just as the cow towns were fading into memory. Through times of "boom and bust," as cattle were driven from one market to another, some towns such as Abilene and Wichita grew into large, thriving cities. Caldwell, Dodge City, and Newton became pleasant, mid-sized cities. A few people got rich, while most managed to support their families comfortably. These towns are now economic centers for the farms and ranches in their regions.

However, many still recall their history as boom towns. Abilene, Wichita, and Dodge have museums in which visitors may still walk the streets and imagine those exciting days when cowboys and their cattle came to town.

Glossary

boomtown—A town that grew up rapidly, usually a mining town or a town where a cattle trail met a railroad line

booster—A person who enthusiastically supports the growth of a town

cattle drive—The herding of cattle from ranches and grazing lands to the railroad lines at cow towns

dime novel—An inexpensive paperback book about the Wild West

dogie—Pronounced with a long *o* as in *own*, a calf with no mother; from the Spanish word *dogal*, a short rope used to keep a calf away from its mother during milking

false front—A wooden front that made a building appear larger

gallows—A wooden structure on which criminals were hanged

livery—Place where horses were fed, watered, and sheltered

mercantile—An early department store; also a general store

necktie social—A hanging in the early days of cow towns

ornery—Irritable, bad-humored

outlaw—A criminal

prospect—To search for gold and other precious materials

quarantine—Isolating people or animals in a place to keep disease from spreading

range—Open grasslands where cattle and horses graze

rustler—A cattle thief

shipping yard—A pen near a railroad station that holds cattle before they are loaded on to railroad cars

sod—Slabs of prairie grass and roots used to make houses and other buildings

tallow—Animal fat used to make soap and candles

vigilante—Someone who takes the law into his or her own hands

Time Line

Texas cattle drives begin. Two thousand cattle are moved from Texas along the Shawnee Trail.

Wild Bill Hickock succeeds Tom Smith as Marshal of Dodge City.

The American Civil War is fought.

On April 15, James Butler Hickock replaces Tom Smith as marshal of Abilene. In July the Santa Fe Railroad extends its line to Newton, Kansas, which becomes the end of the Chisholm Trail.

Kansas becomes a state.

Jesse Chisholm dies at Left Hand Spring near what is now Geary, Oklahoma.

| 1861 | 1862 | 1863 | 1864 | 1865 | 1866 | 1867 | 1868 | 1869 | 1870 | 1871 | 1872 | 1873 |

The U.S. government gives away 128 million acres to the railroads.

More than three million Texas longhorn cattle are driven up the Chisholm Trail to the Union Pacific (later the Kansas Pacific) Railroad shipping yard at Abilene.

The Union Pacific Railroad moves westward. Track is laid at an average rate of one mile per day. The town of Wichita is established. Jesse Chisholm blazes the Chisholm Trail. Major General Grenville M. Dodge orders Captain Henry Pierce to build Fort Dodge.

Joseph G. McCoy builds a shipping yard in Abilene at the end of the Chisholm Trail. The first cattle drive from Texas up the Chisholm Trail arrives.

Ellsworth follows Abilene as the northern shipping point of the Texas cattle trail. A branch of the Santa Fe Railroad arrives at Wichita.

The last Texas cattle arrive in Dodge City. Kansas passes a law banning Texas cattle between March 1 and December 1, the season for the long drives.

Four Kansas railroads ship 122,914 Texas cattle in just eight months.

Dodge City becomes the "Cowboy Capital" of the West.

1874 1875 1876 1877 1878 1879 1880 1881 1882 1883 1884 1885

Most of the herds head for Dodge City, another shipping point on the Santa Fe Railroad line.

Find Out More

Children's Books

Bial, Raymond. *Ghost Towns of the American West.* Boston: Houghton Mifflin, 2001.

Bulloch, Ivan, and Diane James. *I Wish I Were a Cowboy.* Chicago: World Book, 1998.

Duncan, Dayton. *The West: An Illustrated History for Children.* New York: Little, Brown, 1996.

Hicks, Peter, David Antram and David Salariya. *You Wouldn't Want To Live in a Wild West Town!: Dust You'd Rather Not Settle.* New York: Franklin Watts, 2002.

Johmann, Carol A., Elizabeth J. Rieth, and Michael P. Kline. Going West!: *Journey on a Wagon Train to Settle a Frontier Town.* Charlotte, VT: Williamson, 2000.

Kalman, Bobbie. *Boomtowns of the West.* New York: Crabtree, 1999.
————*Homes of the West.* New York: Crabtree, 1999.
————*Who Settled the West?* New York: Crabtree, 1999.

Merker, Meghan, and Nate Brown. *Roll On, Little Dogies: Songs and Activities for Young Cowpokes.* Salt Lake City: Gibbs Smith, 1996.

Stefoff, Rebecca. *Children of the Westward Trail.* Brookfield, CT: Millbrook Press, 1996.

Whitman, Sylvia. *Children of the Frontier.* Minneapolis: Carolrhoda Books, 1998.

Places to Visit

Boot Hill Museum and Front Street
Front Street and Fifth Street
Dodge City, Kansas 67801
phone: (316) 227-8188
www.boothill.org

Chisholm Trail Heritage Center
1000 North 29th Street
Duncan, Oklahoma 73534
phone: (580) 252-6692
www.onthechisolmtrail.com

Jefferson National Expansion
Memorial
(Gateway Arch)
11 North 4th Street
St. Louis, Missouri 63102
phone: (314) 655-1700

Old Abilene Town and Museum
201 Southeast 6th Street
Abilene, Kansas 67410
phone: (785) 263-4194

Old Cow Town Museum
1871 Sim Park Drive
Wichita, Kansas 67203
phone: (316) 264-0671
www.old-cowtown.org

Stuhr Museum
3133 West Highway 34
Grand Island, Nebraska 68801
phone: (308) 385-5316
www.stuhrmuseum.org/index.htm

Selected Web Sites

The American West
www.americanwest.com

Handbook of Texas Online
www.tsha.utexas.edu

Kansas Cattle Towns
www.kansascattletowns.com

The Kansas Collection
www.kancoll.org

New Perspectives on the West:
Cowboys (PBS)
*www.pbs.org/weta/thewest/program/e
pisodes/five/cowboys.htm*

Index

About the Author

The author and illustrator of over eighty books for children and adults, **Raymond Bial** is best known for his versatility in portraiture, landscape, and still-life photography. His photo-essays for children include *Corn Belt Harvest*, *County Fair*, *Amish Home*, *Frontier Home*, *Shaker Home*, *The Underground Railroad*, *Portrait of a Farm Family*, *With Needle and Thread: A Book About Quilts*, *Mist Over the Mountains: Appalachia and Its People*, *Cajun Home*, *One-Room School*, *Where Lincoln Walked*, *Ghost Towns of the American West*, *A Handful of Dirt*, *Tenement: Immigrant Life on the Lower East Side*, and many others. His series of books include Building America and Lifeways, an acclaimed series about Native-American people. He has published three works of fiction for children: *The Fresh Grave and Other Ghostly Stories*, *The Ghost of Honeymoon Creek*, and *Shadow Island*.

He lives in Urbana, Illinois, with his wife and children.